T0062912

Though this is a small collection, it conveys a relevant message about the often forgotten men who fought in Southeast Asia in the 1960s and 70s. The author's emotional connection to these soldiers and their families is obvious and laudable.

—US Review of Books

LETTERS, MEDALS, ROSES

MARJORIE A. BROCKMAN

Letters, Medals, Roses

A collection of poems on the
Vietnam War and the effects on the
Vietnam Veterans and their families

Order this book online at www.trafford.com
or email orders@trafford.com

Most Trafford titles are also available at major online book retailers.

Print information available on the last page.

ISBN: 978-1-4120-9303-3 (sc)
ISBN: 978-1-4251-9687-5 (e)

Trafford rev. 10/16/2015

 www.trafford.com

North America & international
toll-free: 1 888 232 4444 (USA & Canada)
fax: 812 355 4082

Letters, Medals, Roses

A collection of poems on the
Vietnam War and the effects on the
Vietnam Veterans and their families

Marjorie A. Brockman, Author

Contents

TABLE OF CONTENTS

DEDICATION PAGE

This book of poetry is dedicated to all those who have suffered loss in their lives, whether it be to a lost love or a friend or son or daughter lost to a war. Special mention is made herein to the Southeast Side Vietnam Veterans in Chicago, IL. Many of the ideas for the poems within this book came from many hours of listening to these special veterans tell their stories about their Nam experience. They have encouraged me to continue writing. You are holding in your hands the results of their encouragement.

FOREWORD

This book of poetry was written as a result of many hours of conversations with Vietnam Veterans at the Chicago Welcome Home Parade on June 13, 1986, and at several Vietnam veterans' reunions held in Crawfordsville and Kokomo, Indiana over the last several years.

For the reader who is not a veteran, I hope that these poems will give you a better understanding of the problems these veterans faced in the past and are still facing today. For the veteran who reads this book, I hope that my poems will somehow help you as you try to heal the emotional and physical scars caused by this war.

The following is an overview of the collection of poems in this book related to the Vietnam War. These Memories Will Last is a poem that describes how a soldier felt on his way to Vietnam, his fears, his thoughts, his experiences and the impact they would have on his life in the future. All That I Can Give is a poem about the nurses in Vietnam and their dedication to nursing the many wounded soldiers. Missing You is a poem about a boy whose father was killed in Vietnam before his birth. The boy is missing his father and reflecting on how it could have been if his father were here with him today. Other topics covered in my war poems are Agent Orange, veteran suicide, the P.O.W./M.I.A. issue, and the Welcome Home Parade in Chicago, Illinois.

ABOUT THE AUTHOR

Marjorie A. Brockman started writing poetry in her senior year at Lyons Township High School in LaGrange, Illinois, with encouragement from her high school English teacher. Since then, she has dabbled in writing poetry but never felt that the poems were good enough to show anyone. After getting involved with the Vietnam Veterans Welcome Home Parade in Chicago in 1986, she began writing poetry to describe the many emotions expressed and issues raised by the Vietnam War and the veterans' experiences. After showing some of these poems to veterans to see whether the emotions being expressed were on target, she was encouraged to continue writing.

The author has a B.S. Degree in Business (1985) from Elmhurst College, Elmhurst, Illinois, and an M.B.A. from DePaul University (1989), Chicago, IL, and a Certificate of Completion in Managed Care from Benedictine University in Lisle, IL.

She is currently employed at Argonne National Laboratory in the Purchasing Department.

Letters, Medals, Roses

LETTERS, MEDALS, ROSES

Why does a monument
    make so many people cry
And leave letters, medals, roses
    for the people who have died?

What magic power does it hold   5
    that draws the families near
Placing hands on the granite
    on the name that they hold dear.

They linger there for hours
    spending time with their wall name   10
Hugging other family members
    also hurting from the pain.

The magic power that it has
    lies deep within the black.
That warm sensation that they feel   15
    is their loved ones touching back!

THESE MEMORIES WILL LAST

He was only 19 when he said goodbye
to his friends and his Mom and Dad.
He waved goodbye with tears in his eyes
as he stepped into the plane.
The plane was filled with servicemen   5
from everywhere U.S.A.
They talked of home, their Moms, their girls
and the dangers they would face.
But as the plane approached Saigon,
silence filled the air.   10
Some hands shook, some tears fell,
but everyone felt the same.

He reported for duty when he got off the plane,
assigned to the 1ˢᵗ Cavalry.
Fresh out of school and ready to fight,   15
he was trained to the 10ᵗʰ degree.
But compared to the men already there,
he was just an "FNG".
He tried to get close to the guys in his group,
but they wouldn't let it be.   20
They gave him a nickname like Doc or Turk
and said you follow me.

In the jungle for days, he learned to know
the sounds that would bring his death.
His survival instincts took control,   25
and he looked out for his ass.
As each day passed he saw each guy
get hurt or blown away.
So he got like all the others —
scared to death but primed to kill,   30
Counting the days till he could go home
and praying to God each night.

His luck was good; he made it home
and lives a normal life.
Except for the dreams and silent screams   35
and visions of all that death.
His friends tell him to forget it,
because it's in the past.
But forgetting is impossible;
these memories will last.   40

MISSING YOU

We've never met, but I'm your son
    Born while you were in Nam.
They say I look just like you, Dad,
    And I even have your name.

I keep your picture close to me   5
    Every night and day
And ask God why you had to die
    In a place so far away.

I'm angry that you cannot share
    My childhood with me and   10
Teach me how to be the man
    That you'd want me to be.

I love my Mom, but she can't show me
    How to win a fight,
How to pitch a curve ball   15
    Or how to cast just right.

If only I could hold your hand
    And look into your eyes
To hear you laugh, to hear your voice
    Or have you hold me when I cry.   20

But since I know that you are gone
    And won't be coming home,
I'll just have to settle for
    These quiet times alone
Looking at your picture   25
    Thinking how it could have been.

Closeup of Nurses' Memorial in Washington, D.C. Photograph taken by Marjorie Brockman.

Nurses' Memorial, Washington, D. C. Photograph taken by Marjorie Brockman.

ALL THAT I CAN GIVE
TRIBUTE TO THE NURSES

It's nighttime, the sun's gone down,
but the stinking heat remains.
I'm sitting in a hospital tent
holding a soldier's hand.   5
I've been working 24 hours now,
and I'm ready to collapse
But the haunting look in his eyes
gives me the strength to last.
He's hurt so bad and in such pain,   10
and I want to help him live,
But holding his hand and being there
is all that I can give.

All my nurse's training
now just seems to be in vain.   15
I can't help this boy get home alive;
I can only ease his pain.
I try to reassure him
that he's going to be just fine
When deep inside I know   20
he won't make it through to dawn.

So I listen to him tell me
about his family
And how he wants to see
his Mom and Dad so terribly.   25
He makes me promise that, if he dies,
I will write his mother
And tell her that his last words were
how very much he loved her.

So many boys were hurt in Nam,   30
and I took care of them.
I did my best to ease their pain
and comfort like a friend.
Though their numbers were many
and, with time, their names might fade,   35
I will never forget their faces
or the promises I made.

Photograph of Nurses' Memorial,
Washington, D.C.
Taken by Marjorie Brockman.

SORTING IT OUT

The Viet Nam War is over.
They say it's in the past.
Explain that to a veteran
Whose memories still last.

When summer's heat begins to swell,   5
His mind returns to Nam.
A ceiling fan's a chopper, and
That backfiring car's a bomb.
A loved one trying to wake him
Is the enemy at dawn.   10
His hand beneath the pillow
Reaches for the gun.
He wakes in fright
Because it's not there
And now he's going to die.   15
His body pulsates from his pounding heart,
As he sits up in bed and cries.
He can't remember the now from the past.
They both merge in and out.
Isn't someone able to tell him   20
What that war was all about.

He served his country
With honor and pride
And sometimes lost his limbs.
Yet when he returned on the Freedom Bird,   25
His countrymen spat on him
And made him ashamed of the job he'd done
And the uniform that he wore.
So he hid the fact that he fought in Nam
And never talked of it anymore.   30
All those feelings of rejection,
And a terrible sense of loss
Had to be kept within himself
No matter what the cost.

He's spent 30 years trying to sort it out   35
And still cannot see why
58,000 plus young men
From the US had to die.
For them, the war has ended
And they're finally at peace.   40
But, for many Vietnam veterans,
Their battle does not cease.

BROTHER OF MINE
(Dedicated to Dave)

Brother of mine, why did you die?
    If I had been there, I could have
kept you alive
    But I wasn't there. God, why wasn't I there?

I was there, but too late, only to   5
    put your body on the chopper and
take you home for the last time.
    I didn't know you were in Nam
until I rolled your body over in
    the chopper.   10

What do you expect me to say to our
    parents? I'm sorry?
I should've been there! I can't
    face them.
I promised them I would look out   15
    for you, but I didn't.
God why wasn't it me who died
    instead of you?
Please take my life and put his
    back.   20

Brother of mine, how can I live
    Knowing that you are gone.
How do I live with the grief and
    the pain?
How do I move on without you   25
    I'm so lost and so alone!

AGENT ORANGE

While I was on patrol,
a U.S. plane flew by.
I waved at the pilot
and got something in my eyes.
My eyes burned from the chemicals   5
being sprayed on the trees
To defoliate the jungle
and uncover the V.C.
I wish someone had told me
what it would do to me.   10

The chemical's called Agent Orange
and little did I know
That it would cause birth defects
and make cancerous tumors grow.
Those of us who made it home   15
thought we had it made.
Then found out that Agent Orange
would put us in our graves
Or take the sight from our newborns
or leave their limbs deformed.   20

The fighting ended years ago,
yet the dying still goes on.
Will there ever be an end
to the death from Viet Nam!

Photograph of the soldiers' statues
overlooking the Vietnam Veterans Memorial,
Washington, D.C.
Photograph taken by Marjorie A. Brockman.

THE VIETNAM VETERANS MEMORIAL
"THE WALL"

In Washington there is a Wall
made of granite black
In memory of all those men
who never made it back
From Viet Nam, that place of Hell,   5
where they fought and died.
And returned home in coffins
while their families cried.

The Wall is in a quiet place
surrounded by grass and trees   10
And monuments to other greats
in US history.
The difference is those monuments
each honor only one.
The Wall quietly pays tribute to   15
fifty-eight thousand some,
Who made the ultimate sacrifice
by giving up their lives
To serve their country with
courage, devotion, and pride.   20

As well as a memorial
to all those men who died,
The Wall is a healing place
for loved ones left behind.
The faces of the people   25
who are searching for a name
Are reflected on the Wall's
Mirror-like shine
And when they find the name
that they've been searching for,   30
The Wall's surface
also reflects their pain.

The knowledge that a loved one
is forever gone
Becomes reality   35
when seen etched in granite stone.
So they kneel in prayer, cry,
and ask each other why
Their sons, husbands, fathers
were the ones that had to die.   40
They wipe their tears, stand with pride,
then slowly walk away
Vowing to remember them
in their prayers each day.

WASTED TALENT

It's summertime and the sidewalks steam
    from the summer sun.
A veteran sits in the corner of a room
    and in his hand's a gun.
He's contemplating using it   5
    and taking his own life.
The only thing that's stopping him
    is thoughts of his wife.

Things haven't been the same
    since he returned from Nam.   10
He can't forget the screams, the pain,
    the death, the bombs.
And then he starts to drink
    when the flashbacks get too bad
So he fights with his wife   15
    and makes his kids real sad.
His family says he's changed
    from the man they used to know.
He's introverted and moody
    and won't let his feelings show.   20
He hasn't kept a job
    longer than one month.

He says they're just not interesting;
    they don't provide the rush.
So, alone, depressed and drunk,   25
    this soldier sings a song,
Raises the gun close to his head
    and helps his death along.

SOUTHEAST SIDE VIETNAM VETS CADENCE

Take a look as we march by
    We're Vietnam vets from the Southeast Side.
We love this country, yes indeed.
    We fought in Nam to keep her free.
And if we had to we would fight   5
    Once again for what is right.

See this flag we hold above.
    That's our flag, the one we love.
Don't ever let it touch the dirt
    Or you'll be in for a world of hurt.   10

Please try to understand that we
    Have seen some pretty terrible things.
Many of our buddies died
    Right in front of our very eyes.

Many of our guys are still   15
    Locked in cages against their will.
It's up to us to set them free
    And bring them home to family.
P.O.W./M.I.A.
    They're in our hearts and prayers each day.   20

Hey, hey, what d'ya say
  What d'ya think of us today.
Veterans of the Southeast Side
  Marching proudly side by side.
It's 40 years since we've come home.   25
  Let us know we're not alone.
If you care, then let us know
  Stand up now and let it show.

CHICAGO WELCOME HOME PARADE

JUNE 13, 1986

June 13 I won't soon forget
    Nor will thousands of our vets.
You ask, what happened on that day?
    The Vietnam Veterans Welcome Home Parade.   5

Many of Chicago's streets
    Were filled with soldiers' marching feet.
Walking tall, marching proud,
    Calling out their cadence loud.
Army, Navy, Air Force, Marines   10
    Some in uniform, some in jeans.
Some with medals, some with none.
    Some in wheelchairs with their legs gone.

War buddies hugged and cried
    Man, they said, I thought you died.   15
Gold star mothers with tears in their eyes
    Marched with pictures of their sons who died.
Floats drove by with men in cages
    For the POWs whose war still wages.

25

If all the tears that fell that day   20
    Could have been collected in some way
There'd be enough water to fill an ocean
    From the tremendous outpouring of emotion.

The crowds that gathered grew and grew
    Holding banners saying We love You.   25
Ticker tape flew through the air
    To show the vets Chicago cares.

MICHAEL

When I heard his first cry
    on the day he was born
I knew I was especially blessed
    With a gift from the Lord
to cherish and love.   5
    He would bring us much happiness.

I named him Michael, my blue-eyed boy
    With a smile that would melt your heart.
We were bonded from that very day
    And nothing could tear us apart.   10

I helped him to walk
    and rocked him to sleep
When the "ghost" in his room kept him up.
    I played peek-a-boo
and went to the zoo.   15
    I nursed him through measles and mumps.

When he was 19, I kissed him goodbye
    As his plane left for Viet Nam.
He looked so fine in his uniform.
    He made us so very proud.   20

Don't worry, he said, I'm not afraid.
    I'll be home within the year.
So dry your tears and give me a smile
    And forget all of your fears.

My very worst fear that he would be killed   25
    Became a reality.
And all the tears that I could spill
    Would not bring him home to me.

With time, I have learned
    to thank the good Lord   30
For giving him to me
    To cherish and love and be so proud of
Because he died so we could be free.

I'll never forget you , Michael, my son
    So handsome and so tall.   35
It's better to have had you awhile
    Than to not have had you at all.

GONE NOT FORGOTTEN

I wear a red bracelet on my wrist
    With the name of a vet on the missing list.
Randall J. Nightingale, AX2.
    His friends called him Randy; his family did too.

He was lost over water in North Viet Nam and   5
    No body was every found.
P.O.W./M.I.A.?
    No one knows even today.

I pray for the day when his fate is known
    And either way we can bring him home   10
To unite with his family or to rest in peace,
    So the pain and suffering will finally cease.

So I'll wear this bracelet on my wrist
    Until Randy's no longer on that list.
Gone not forgotten, this M.I.A.   15
    He's in my heart and prayers each day.

AX2 RANDALL J. NIGHTINGALE
USN 3/17/68 NVN/OW

CEASE FIRE

His eyes look at you,
but he does not see.

His mind is far away,
where survival is the game.

He's still there, stuck in time,   5
unable to crawl away
From the continuous playing
film of horrors in his mind
Of jungle smells, chopper sounds,
rifle bursts and people's screams.   10

Until the screams he hears are his.

Suddenly, something warm and firm
has grasped his arm.

Although not able to relate,
instinct tells him this presence   15
Is here to help, calm, soothe.

He senses he's not alone
and feels safe -- CEASE FIRE!

IRREVERENT THOUGHTS

Day one in the Nam
What a terrible sight
Blood and guts of a friend
Who just lost the fight.
Say goodbye to that GI   5
No more will he live.
Say a prayer, put him in a bag
And send his body home.

Wood coffins piled high
Waiting for a flight   10
Destination graveyard
Hometown USA.
Home to waiting families
Who'll now be alone.

Stinking heat, fungus feet   15
Monsoon rain and mud
Boonie hats, giant rats
That grenade's a dud.

Combat boots, many gooks
Crawling underground   20
Piles of shit, pungi sticks
A body has been found.

Someone's fragged, body bags
For the many parts
U.S. Marines with MI6s   25
Never leave their dead.

Navy Seals, gourmet meals
Right out of a can
Huey choppers, weapon boppers
War artillery.   30

Freedom bird, freedom bird
Take me far away
From the heat, the death, the pain
Take me home again.

Lift me up very high   35
In the shelter of your wings
Take me home to Mom and Dad
And more pleasant things.

DRAFTED

Uncle Sam wants your son
    To fight the war in Nam
Not declared, but it's a war
    With real fighting going on.
We're losing men left and right   5
    To the weapons of V.C.
We need replacements for these guys
    And your son looks good to me.
Only 19? That's OK. He will fit the bill.
    You can be sure when his time is through   10
We'll send him on home to you.

Only nineteen, still in blue jeans
    Wet behind the ears.
Send him far away to a place called Hue
    And make him cry real tears.   15
Cause he's scared as hell that he'll get killed
    On his very first Nam day.
Issue him a gun, tell him to run
    And stay well out of sight.
He's no dope but hasn't learned the ropes   20
    On how not to get shot.
New guys usually get shot
    Within their first few days.
So let him take point
    And di di on up the road.   25

ANTICIPATION

A soldier dressed in khakis
    slowly walks up to the Wall.
He finds the name of his best friend
    engraved in granite there.
He reaches out to lay his hand   5
    on his best friend's name
And bows his head in silence
    as he tries to fight the pain
He's afraid of the emotions
    kept so deep and tight inside.   10
He doesn't want to break down.
    He doesn't want to cry.
Cause once he starts,
    there will be no end
to the tears he's kept inside.   15
    His eyes are welling up with tears,
and he tries desperately not to cry.
    He turns his head side to side
to see who's standing by
    Because he doesn't want to let   20
anyone see him cry.
    But finally he falls to his knees
and just starts to sob
    As memories flow of that fatal day
in which his friend was lost.   25

How can someone who lived life large
    just disappear from view
With no time to straighten his affairs
    or say his last goodbyes.
Why did this happen to his friend and   30
    not to him?
He should have disappeared too.

Hey soldier, go ahead - It's OK to cry.
    Tears are like medicine.
They'll help you heal the scars.   35
    So don't try to hold them back
Just let your feelings show.
    Put your arms around someone
And let those tears just flow.
    Just think of them as raindrops   40
Slowly cleansing as they fall
    All the pain you've held inside yourself.

COLORS OF FREEDOM

Red, white and blue
    Colors of freedom
Flown proudly over stadiums,
    Buildings, schools
Waved by the wind   5
    Pledged to by children and adults
Raised with pomp to honor
    Olympic medals
Carried proudly by veterans
    marching in parades,   10
Held high, never touch the ground
    Carried in a soldier's shirt
while in the heat of battle
    Bleeds red from a wounded
soldier's blood.   15
    Draped over coffins of
veterans who have given
    the ultimate sacrifice
Folded in a triangle and handed
    to the mother, wife/husband of the   20
honored veteran.

Flown proudly in the yard of the
      fallen veteran by his/her family.
to honor his/her service and their loss.
      Properly burned and honored   25
when its stripes are torn and tattered.
      Only to be replaced by a new one

LIST OF PHOTOGRAPHS

All of the photographs included in this book were taken by the author. Permission was obtained to include the cover photograph in a letter from Gilbert M. Ortiz, Secretary of Southeast Side Vietnam Veterans. Permission was obtained verbally from Katherine of Vietnam Veterans Memorial Permit office to use photographs taken by the author of Nurses' Memorial, Vietnam Veterans Memorial and Three (3) Statues used in this book.

The following photographs are included:

1. Cover. Mural in South Chicago across from Our Lady of Guadalupe Parish, owned and maintained by Chicago Southeast Side Vietnam Veterans.
2. Page 8 - Close-ups of Nurses' Memorial in Washington, D.C.
3. Page II - Nurses' Memorial in Washington, D.C.
4. Page 18 - Three soldiers overlooking Vietnam Veterans Memorial in Washington, D.C.
5. Back Cover - photographs of specific panels on the Vietnam Veterans Memorial in Washington, D.C. to remember the names of Thomas P. Cadieux and Wayne S. Zach, both killed in action.

COVER PHOTOGRAPHS

The photograph on the front cover of this book is a photograph taken by the author of a memorial on the wall of a building in South Chicago, Illinois. It is owned by the Chicago Southeast Side Vietnam Veterans and maintained by them. It contains all of the names of the veterans who were killed or missing in action from the State of Illinois. Above the memorial are pictures of twelve (12) special veterans who all were killed in Vietnam and are the most recorded number of veterans killed in Vietnam from one parish.

The photographs on the back cover were also taken by the author of two specific panels on the Vietnam Veterans Memorial in Washington, D.C. The first picture clearly shows the name of Thomas P. Cadieux, a soldier who was killed in Vietnam by friendly fire. He worked at the same company, Grayhill, Inc., with the author in LaGrange, Illinois.

The second photograph on the back cover was specifically taken for the name Wayne S. Zach. He was from the town of Brookfield, Illinois and was killed in action. He was a family friend.

Printed in the United States
By Bookmasters